Index

ISBN: 978-0-7877-2169-5

Cover organ photograph courtesy of Rodgers Instruments, LLC. Used by permission.

A Lorenz Company • www.lorenz.com

'Tis the Spring of Saints Today

(Come, Ye Faithful, Raise the Strain)

Sw.   Trumpet 8
Gt.   Principals 8, 4
Ped. Principals 16, 8

Richard A. Williamson
Tune: ST. KEVIN
by Arthur Seymour Sullivan

Duration: 2:10

70/1958L-2

4

My Jesus, I Love Thee

Sw. Flute 8, Flute or String Celeste 8
Gt.   Principals 8, 2
Ped. Soft 16, 8, Sw. to Ped.

Mark Hayes
Arranged by **Douglas E. Wagner**
Tune: GORDON
by **Adoniram J. Gordon**

Duration: 3:50

6

70/1958L-6

8

70/1958L-9

Variants on "Now the Green Blade Riseth"

Gt.   Foundations 8, 4, 2
Ped. 16, 8, Gt. to Ped.

Robert Lau
Tune: **NOËL NOUVELET**
Traditional French melody

Duration: 1:55

Come, Sweet Death

Sw. Light Solo Reed 8
Gt.   Strings 8, 4
Ped. Light 16, 8, Sw. to Ped.

Edward Broughton
Tune: KOMM, SÜSSER TOD
by **Johann Sebastian Bach**

Duration: 4:15

14

Sing Hosannas to the King!

Sw. Principals 8, 4, 2, Reeds 8, 4
Gt.   Principals 8, 4, 2, Sw. to Gt.
Ped. Principals 16, 8, Sw. to Ped.

Lani Smith

Duration: 1:30

Festivity on "Come, Thou Fount"

Sw. Bright Reed 8
Gt. Foundations 8, 4, 2
Ped. 16, 8, Gt. to Ped.

Douglas E. Wagner
Tune: NETTLETON
from Wyeth's *Repository of Sacred Music*, 1813

Duration: 1:50

What Wondrous Love Is This

Sw. String 8
Gt. Flute 8
Ped. Flutes 16, (8)

Anna Laura Page
Tune: **WONDROUS LOVE**
from *Southern Harmony*, 1835

Duration: 3:00

22

No Ped.

Postlude on "Irish"

Sw.   Flutes 8, 4, (2)
Gt.   Principal 8
Ped. Gedeckt 16, 8

Lani Smith
Tune: IRISH
from *Hymns and Sacred Poems* (1749)

Duration: 1:45

A little slower ♩ = ca. 112

Agnus Dei
from "Requiem"

Sw.   Strings and Flutes 8, 4
Gt.   Diapason 8, Sw. to Gt.
Ped. Bourdon 16, Sw. to Ped.

Wolfgang Amadeus Mozart
Arranged by **Christopher Gale**

Duration: 2:25

Softly and Tenderly

Sw. Light Reed 8
Gt.   Warm Flutes 8, 4, Flute Celeste 8
Ped. Soft 16, Gt. to Ped.

Dan Forrest
Arranged by **Douglas E. Wagner**
Tune: THOMPSON
by **Will L. Thompson**

Duration: 2:55

32

Throned Upon the Awful Tree

Sw. Foundations 8, 4, 2
Gt. Principals 8, 4, Flutes 8, 4
Ped. 16, 8, Sw. to Ped., Gt. to Ped.

Lyndell Leatherman
Tune: **ARFON**
Traditional Welsh melody

* Introduction and ending adapted from *Prelude and Fugue in G Minor* (Johann Sebastian Bach).

Duration: 2:05

Guide Me, O Thou Great Jehovah

Sw. Bright Reed 8
Gt.   Foundations 8, 4, 2
Ped. 16, 8, Gt. to Ped.

Dan Forrest
Arranged by **Douglas E. Wagner**
Tune: CWM RHONDDA
by **John Hughes**

Duration: 3:25

www.lorenz.com
JD

38

O Bless the Lord, My Soul!

Sw. Strings 8, 4
Gt.   Flutes 8, 4
Ped. Light 16, Sw. to Ped.

Jason W. Krug
Tune: ST. THOMAS
by **Aaron Williams**

Duration: 2:30

42

Toccata on "Solemnis Haec Festivas"

Sw.   Principals 8, 4
Gt.   Principals 8, 4, 2, Sw. to Gt.
Ped. Principals 16, 8, Sw. to Ped.

Tom Birchwood
Tune: SOLEMNIS HAEC FESTIVAS
from *Graduale*, 1685

Duration: 1:50

46

Gradually increase registration (crescendo pedal)

46

Gradually increase registration (crescendo pedal)

Variants on "St. Magnus"

Sw. Flute 8
Gt.   Flutes 8, 4, Strings 8, 4
Ped. Light 16, 8, Gt. to Ped.

Stephen Walters
Tune: ST. MAGNUS
by **Jeremiah Clarke**

Duration: 3:10

48

50

Meditation on "Ubi Caritas"

Sw. Light Reed 8
Gt. Flutes 8, 4
Ped. 16, Gt. to Ped.

Douglas E. Wagner
Tune: **UBI CARITAS**
Traditional plainsong

Duration: 2:00

Go Joyfully

Sw. Flutes 8, 4
Gt.   Principals 8, 4
Ped. Principal 8

Richard A. Williamson

No Ped.

Ped.

Duration: 2:05

54

Sarabande

(From *Suite No. 6 in D Major* for Unaccompanied Cello)

Sw. Light Strings 8
Gt. Principal 8
Ped. Light 16, 8, Sw. to Ped.

Johann Sebastian Bach
Arranged by **Christopher Gale**

Duration: 2:00

When Peace Like a River

Sw. Flute 8, String 8
Gt. Principal 8
Ped. 16, Sw. to Ped.

Douglas E. Wagner
Tune: VILLE DU HAVRE
by **Philip B. Bliss**

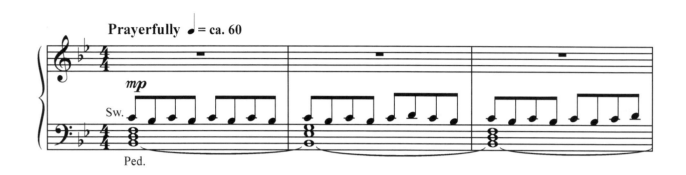

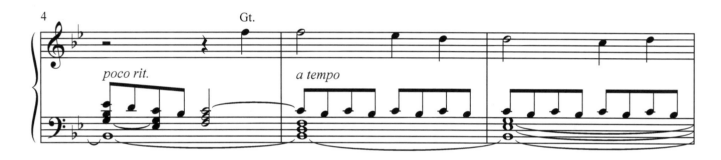

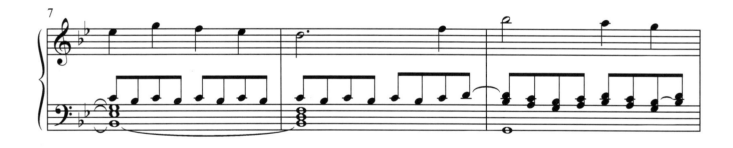

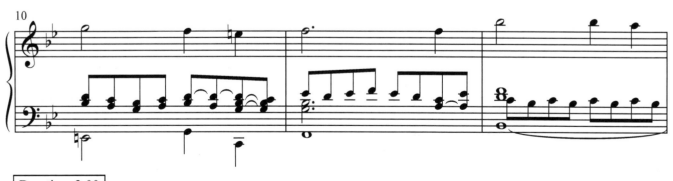

Duration: 2:00

Saints Bound for Heaven

Sw. Flutes 8, 4, 2
Gt. Principals 8, 4
Ped. Bourdon 16, 8

Edward Broughton
Tune: SAINTS BOUND FOR HEAVEN
from *Southern Harmony*, 1834

Duration: 1:45

The King of Love My Shepherd Is

I. Sw. Light Flutes 8, 4   **II. Sw.** Flutes and Strings 8, 4
Gt. Warm Solo 8
Ped. Soft 16, Sw. to Ped.

Victor Johnson
Tune: ST. COLUMBA
Traditional Irish melody

No Ped.

Duration: 2:25

64

70/1958L-64

Postlude on "St. Patrick's Breastplate"

Sw.   Bright Reeds 8, 4
Gt.   Principals 8, 4
Ped. Principals 16, 8, Gt. to Ped.

Lani Smith
Tune: ST. PATRICK'S BREASTPLATE
Traditional Irish melody

Duration: 2:10

In the Shadow of the Almighty

Sw.   Strings 8, 4
Ped. Dulciana 16, Sw. to Ped.

Christina Becket

Duration: 1:30

God of Our Fathers

Sw. Strings and Flutes 8, 4
Gt. Principals 8, 4, 2
Ped. Principals 16, 8

Lani Smith
Tune: NATIONAL HYMN
by **George William Warren**

Duration: 3:00

www.lorenz.com

72

70/1958L-72

No Ped.

Ped.

rit.

Slower

rit.

74

Deep River
(from *American Rhapsody*)

Sw. String 8, String Celeste 8
Gt. Flutes 8, 4, Sw. to Gt.
Ped. Soft 16, 8 Sw. to Ped.

Pietro A. Yon
Tune: DEEP RIVER
Arranged by **Michael Ryan**

Duration: 2:15

70/1958L-74

JD

Rejoice, Ye Pure in Heart

Sw. Bright Reeds 8, 4
Gt.   Full 8, 4, 2
Ped. 16, 8, Gt. to Ped.

Doulas E. Wagner
Tune: MARION
by **Arthur H. Messiter**

Duration: 1:45

We Walk By Faith

Sw. Flutes 8, 4, and/or String Celeste 8
Gt. Principals 8, 4
Ped. 16, 8, Gt. to Ped.

Gregory Hoepfner
Tune: DUNLAP'S CREEK
by **Samuel McFarland**

Duration: 2:50

www.lorenz.com

JD

In Quiet Faith

Sw.   Strings 8, 4
Gt.   Solo Flute 8
Ped. Light 16, 8

Edward Broughton
Tunes: **TRUST IN JESUS,** by **William J. Kirkpatrick** and
OLIVET, by **Lowell Mason**

Duration: 3:15

84

Grand Choeur Dialogué

Sw. Foundations 8, 4, 2, Light Reed 8
Gt. Foundations 8, 4, 2, Mixture, Sw. to Gt.
Ped. Foundations 16, 8, 4, Gt. to Ped.

Eugène Gigout (1844-1925)
Arranged by **Robert Lau**

Duration: 2:40

86

Original registration

70/1958L-86

We Sing to Thee, Thou Son of God

Sw. Strings 8, 4, Flutes 8, 4
Gt. Light Solo Reed 8
Ped. Light 16, Sw. to Ped. 8

James Southbridge

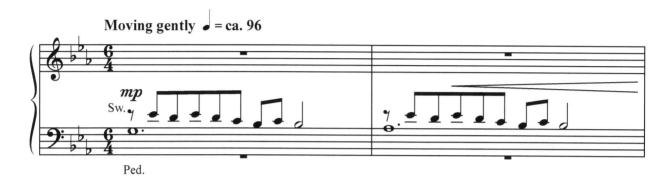

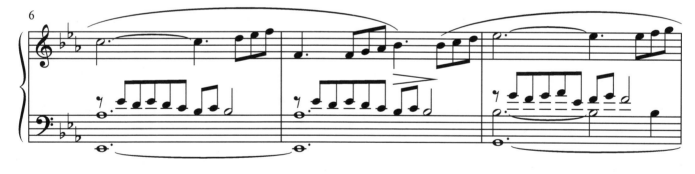

Duration: 3:15

JD

90

Be Thou My Vision

Sw. Oboe 8
Gt. Flutes 8, 4, Flute Celeste 8
Ped. Soft 16, Gt. to Ped.

Dan Forrest
Arranged by **Douglas E. Wagner**
Tune: SLANE
Traditional Irish melody

Duration: 2:50

94

70/1958L-94

Go Your Way with Rejoicing!

Sw. Bright Reed 8
Gt.   Full 8, 4, 2
Ped. 16, 8, Gt. to Ped.

Douglas E. Wagner

Duration: 1:15

There Is No Name So Sweet

Sw. Light Strings 8, 4
Gt. Solo Flute 8
Ped. Dulciana 16, 8

Christina Becket
Tune: **GOLDEN CHAIN**
by **William B. Bradbury**

Duration: 2:15

70/1958L-98

100

Trusting Jesus

Even when my faith is small, trusting Jesus, that is all.

Sw. Light Reed 8
Gt. Strings 8, 4
Ped. Soft 16, Gt. to Ped.

Mary McDonald
Tune: **TRUSTING JESUS**
by **Ira D. Sankey**

Duration: 2:50

Gt. +Flute 8

Two Interludes

Man. Light Flutes 8, (4) and/or String Celeste 8
Ped. Soft 16

Caleb Simper
Arranged by **Michael Ryan**